Table of content

Introduction

There are many books that promise to tell us how to find love. This book is different. It won't tell you what strategy to use. It is dedicated to celebrating love with you – in a meditative space.

Most pieces of music – from Mozart's refined melodies to the catchy tunes that try to cheer us up in the supermarket - revolve around love in all its bliss and its drama. We usually think of love in its romantic sense, experiencing all-encompassing waves of excitement in the early stages of a budding romance, and crushing waves of disappointment when our relationships do not live up to the expectations we have created. We wish for it to fulfill the deep longing for completeness and connectedness which we sense in our hearts. We can spend a whole lifetime chasing after what we believe love should look like.

The intention of this book is to transmit a broader, deeper and more elaborate idea of what love is or can be, beyond the stereotypes or our conditioned ideas of it. It provides a contemplative and practical path to opening ourselves to the deeper, multi-faceted experience of love. The substance of what love really is can be difficult to grasp.

We express our love in endless ways – this is what makes humans so
beautiful. How a newborn loves their mother as the provider of care
differs greatly from the ever-deepening love two adults can have for
each other; it differs from friendship, eros or agape, the transcendent,
purest form of love; it differs from how the earth nourishes all creatu-
res and from how the stars brighten up our nights.

In this book you will find 50 short poems, each a poetic transmission
of 50 faces of love. The poems are connected to one another to build
a story of self-discovery. It is also a meditative manual on the path
towards an abundant experience of love.

I lived this book through storms and sunshine and wrote it
during a six month sailing trip in the Mediterranean – Italy, Croa-
tia, Greece. The text can also be understood as a poetic reflection of
aspects of this journey and adventure. Equally, it could be read as the
story of a woman and a man living together very closely on a sailing
boat – and on the adventure of their relationship under these

conditions. The pictures you will find with some of the poems illustrate certain shades of love from an additional angle and are intended to offer you a further, non-verbal window into love in its many dimensions.

I believe it is part of the human experience to, at times, feel isolated from others or disconnected from love. And yet, in it's deeper expression, love is ever present. You can use each poem to consciously ground yourself in this truth. The fabric of life is accessible to you.

The „50 Shades of Love" presented here are also intended to inspire you to find the very unique fragrances of love which live in your precious heart. It can be one of our most fulfilling and meaningful adventures to discover the full spectrum of love and to enjoy how it expresses itself in our own life and in our shared lives.

This is the journey I am inviting you to embark on with me in this book.

How to use
this book

My first suggestion is to slow down and take a moment to create space
for yourself, your inner experience, and the book.

To really benefit from the content of the poems, you need to read and
sense between the lines.

Take the time to notice how what you read or see affects you inside.

Sometimes new impulses reach us easily; sometimes they touch our
outer shell which might protect our inner softness or vulnerability.
Move through the text slowly.
Do not push things to crack open – the warmth inside will find its
own pace and timing to melt frozen places and allow for new
experiences.

These poems come from softness.

You can read the poems cover-to-cover or take a random verse, following your own intuition and pace; either way will lead you to a deeper understanding of love. I recommend that you read small sections at a time and give yourself space.

The 50 shades presented here are available to you to nourish your heart and soul and to encourage you to continue your own journey of love with courage and delight.

50 Shades
of Love

Departure

I feel as tender as the skin of my lower back,
as soft as the hollow spaces along my vertebrae
which remind me of the trembling nostrils of young
horses.

We embark on our journey.

My body is steadily swayed by the waves.

Wind and sea capriciously begin washing my soul.

The essential will remain.

1. Spaciousness

My breathing spans the space
from the horizon to my tender lungs.
My alveoli reach out to the sun.

This earth is big enough
to hold my inner agitation
in the vastness of its space.

2. The Pureness of a Jump

Dolphins emerge suddenly from the depths of the sea.

Splash!

Everything is permeated by their energy.

There is no boundary between their joy and mine.

3. The paintbrush of the Goddess

My eyes feel like they are melting,
massaged by shades of turquoise and blue.

How many stunning shades of beauty
does the Goddess spoil us with
as she gifts us with her colour palette?

This is love.

4. We dare to have an adventure, together

We move further out.
The waves are high.

I am taking a risk, by depending on you.
You are taking a risk, by depending on me.

My heart flutters, as if I were a butterfly
on it's very first flight.

Is safety ever a given?

5. Magic arises out of the Blue

Water.
This is me.

Slowly, my worn-out thoughts, perceptions and reactions surface into my consciousness.
I wonder, are they loosening from my body?

I am more than what I hear, see or feel.
I am more than my thoughts.

Now I have a chance to swim in open spaces.
I wait. I dive. I breathe in the colour azure, deeply.
This is a space from which I can create.

6. Tenderness

The warm breeze kisses my naked skin.

Hardened places inside me look up in surprise.

Keep kissing, they whisper, keep kissing.

You remind us of once upon a time.

7. Stillness behind the Stage

Stormy gusts of wind fill our sails.

Every muscle in my body tenses up.

I am sure that this is too much for me.

At the same time as I struggle with the wild wind,

I experience a ground of peace.

8. Animal Time Zone

The dolphins are back.

Is this a dolphin family?

They slide through the water in synchronicity
at the same time as they draw arcs into the sea.

They move too quickly for me to fully take them in
despite their seemingly very slow pulse.
They faithfully ride the exhale of the earth.

9. Freaking out and sliding in

You are driving me crazy.

You are making me nervous.

It's enough! I want to go home.

My breathing feels laboured. I experience my craziness,
my edginess, my blaming of the other more fully.

I judge my heart for smiling kindly
when what I really am experiencing is discomfort.
Then suddenly, something cracks inside me and I surrender.

10. Cliffs-Surprise

The cliffs at Kalamaki take me into their arms
in an intimate embrace, as if we have been friends
for ever.

Suddenly, a flash of white light arises from their midst
and imbues the space.

I am bathed and washed with their clarity.
The cliffs shift in my consciousness.

I enjoy their Aliveness*.

*Capitals indicate divine consciousness.

11. Body Appetite

I want to taste your arm. I want to taste your chest
and your belly. This is only for a start.

I want to taste you with my nostrils
and with the vellus hairs that cover my skin.

I will keep my teeth under control
so as not to devour you.

I am just searching for You* in you.

Don't worry about your existence, you will survive.
I desire the real You.

*Capitals indicate divine consciousness.

12. Trust

It seems that you really do exist
and that you keep permeating my life.
It seems that I really do exist
and that I keep permeating your life. Wow!

I experience trembling in the anxious backyard of my heart.

It wants a guarantee, as I risk revealing myself to you.

What can I lean on in order to feel secure?

I suddenly realize that there is an internal safety
that will lead me safely over the ocean.
I feel relief.

13. More Appetite

I simply want You.

Fully.

In all aspects.

Everywhere.

14. The promising Door

You are behaving strangely. Are you pushing me away?

Is this a rejection? Pain arises from within me.

It strikes me that this might not be rejection.

I choose to take the door of belonging.

I love both you and me.

15. Gratitude

You are breathing

in the cathedral

of my heart.

16. Communion I

A tree and a tree and a tree.
Each is unique. Each is centered.

We are initiating and inhabiting
a shared space of love,
the vibrations of which oscillate
as would harmonic chords.

There is no thing to do.
There is no thing to achieve.
There is so much to enjoy.

17. Communion II

We rest in open silence.

We are silence.

18. Communion III

We float in the enlivening joy

that emerges

from this task that we share.

We create together.

19. Rally on the Bottom of the Sea

I recognize You.

You recognize Me.

Bliss moves through my veins.

20. Just Watching

A new program on TV?

I watch the sea.

That is all that I need to exist.

Life happens without my needing to add anything to it.

21. Divine Facts

I feel so happy that I exist.

I feel so happy that you exist.

Joy sparkles within my bones.

22. Philia I

I know we can work things out.

Yesterday, I felt lost and thought that we could not.

You remembered, and you found me.

Hey man, how cool is that.

23. Philia II

I know we can work things out.

Yesterday, you lost yourself and disappeared,

although not from my radar.

Yes we can, honey, yes we can.

We can have fun together again like baby elephants

splashing water around in a pond at sunset.

24. Philia III

Fuck, it seems that I can really rely on you!

I can rely on you.

25. Eros I

Your body seems to be whispering

poems throughout the night.

My ears prick up.

26. Eros II

The tender breeze of your kiss

opens my roses to the light.

27. Eros III

Today, I'm busy.

Our bodies are becoming as delicious as chocolate.

I am eating chocolate.

Chocolate with mint.

28. Forgiveness

My heart trembles.

My warrior wants to take revenge.

This is how I shield my grief.

Eons later, I am ready for my choice.

I want to live in softness.

I finally release you.

I release myself. Freedom.

29. I align into You

The sea might be roaring,

I feel safe.

Ο ΤΑΞΙΑΡΧΗΣ ΜΙΧΑΗΛ

30. Stepping in

Stop.

Stop your addiction to judgement.

It devalues you and others.

Stop it NOW.

31. Harmony

I look at you with the highest regard.

I look at myself with the highest regard.

32. Presence in
the Absence

I can't feel you. I see your beauty,
yet I feel marooned at sea.
I call your name, yet today it creates no resonance.

I notice that I am talking to one whom I think is absent.
Sometimes it's tough.
You touch a string in me.
Nothing ever gets lost.

I slowly recall the delicious playlist of your water music.

33. Will to live

I keep hearing Your call.

34. Zest for Life

I swing myself

into the juiciness of this world.

35. Eros V

I feel you sending missives of joy into my garden.

I am watering the flowers.

36. Break-through

First time sitting up.

First time taking a step.

First time sailing through a thunderstorm.

First time speaking out

that which feels so vulnerable and secret.

At any moment we can birth ourselves into a new world.

37. Fusion

I take in your beauty

and dissolve.

38. Dreaming

Sway with me,

swirl with me,

into infinity.

39. In Embrace

Just as the apple core holds the seed,

the seashell holds the pearl,

the bird's nest holds the chicks,

the soil holds the forest,

the water holds the swimming ducks,

the basins of the earth hold the oceans

and the atmosphere holds the planet,

so my body longs to contain you.

40. Intimacy I

My breathing and I are as close as we can be.

Suddenly,

I am Air.

41. Intimacy II

We are Air.

42. Kermet's time-out

We keep recycling the drama.

We role play as puppets

compelled to entertain old men.

I hope the angels are watching with compassionate eyes.

Let's not forget, out there, there is a field.

The show passes and we will rest together.

43. Volupté

Why would I pick up a piece of paper

when I can choose to have a peach?

44. Caring

Tell me,

my friend,

what feeds your Soul most profoundly?

45. Continuum

I swim in a
turquoise
ocean.

The waters
welcome me
as their's.

There is
instant
embrace.

There is
instant
recognition.

We are one.

46. Fo-rest

Wet roots between green moss.

Your humidity drives me crazy.

I am in bliss, while entangled with you.

47. Inspiration

Drops of Divine Nectar

pop up in my universe

like stars in the night sky.

Will I be able to decode their delicate geometry?

48. Body Enthusiasm I

I have become a soft and sensual being
imbued by the playfulness
of the moon entertaining the Goddess.

Why did it take me so long to see this?

49. Body
Enthusiasm II

I love your playful slides

and especially the carousel.

Shall we go swirling?

50. Beyond

Whatever the shape of the wave,

this boat fits the ocean

perfectly.

I vibrate

in every cell.

Arrival

I feel as tender as the skin of my lower back,
as soft as the hollow spaces along my vertebrae
which remind me of the trembling nostrils of young horses.

My body is deliciously swayed by the waves.

I trust.

About the Author

Nina Koren, MSc, MA, PhD, born in Austria, is an author, trainer and counsellor specialising in body-mind-spirit integration and embodiment training.

Supporting holistic transformation towards health and wellbeing is one of her major passions. Nina loves guiding explorations into our deepest selves, which hold our highest joy and potential. In her healing work she applies a variety of modalities, from transformative talk and meditative dance to gentle healing touch. She provides in-depth process facilitation and supervision for individuals, groups and teams both in private practice in Austria and internationally.
Nina is also the co-founder and director of the inter-connect.me training programs, dedicated to supporting connectedness in relationships and communications.

Contact

For sessions or trainings or to share about your experience of the love shades, you can contact Nina Koren through:

praxis@nina-koren.at

www.nina-koren.at
www.inter-connect.me

Acknowledgements

Those whom I love, know that I love them.

I wish to express my gratitude to Blanche Shahbaghlian for her sensitive, delicate, and beautiful editing of the 50 Shades of Love text.

Many thanks to Carina Steinegger for artfully creating the design of this book, and to Philippa Slade for precious help with further editing.

Deep gratitude also to the Mediterranean Sea, my inspiration.
Thank you for hosting and thoroughly teaching me.

www.ingramcontent.com/pod-product-compliance
Lightning Source LLC
LaVergne TN
LVHW071524180726
843512LV00014B/1158